A place for you, the end of days

A place for you, the end of days

❖

Clem Suder

To order additional copies of this book, contact:
Xlibris
844-714-8691
www.Xlibris.com
Orders@Xlibris.com
842267

CONTENTS

CHAPTER 1

I am trying to find the right words tell you what I have seen. In order to do that I know you will want to know a little about me and how I arrive at conclusions as I see them. When I was a child I was in a family that was going through a divorce, as a consequence my older sister and I were sent to live with my grandparents. It was there on their farm I had what was probably my first experience dealing with something that I would later wonder about. As I played in the creek bed down by the barn I felt as though I was playing with someone. It was the light not really another person, but it felt like one. And I remember feeling as if it seemed to reinforce what they were saying. To me it was all factual. We did not come from a particularly religious family or, I was young to comprehend what was religious in life whenever I was in real desperate need, I would remember that feeling voice that said I am with you always. I know there are times I question my own thoughts, but I am, a that kind of person. I thought if I needed to know something I would. I went through life trying to get by and not allow things to cause too many questions when I needed to know I did.

After many years and experience I was successful and had a job I enjoyed I was doing well. I had a traumatic brain injury. It was quite unlike any kind of injury I had experienced in the past, and I had had quite a few including near death. It knocked me down and kept me down for about seven years I would describe my condition as that of a zombie. I could not originate cognizant thought. I could do what someone asked me to but I had great difficulty in simple problem solving. As I began slowly to improve what seemed the most affected was my memory. The only thing I can say sustained me and kept me thinking was that promise, I am with you always. It was because of that inside I prayed for help for what I think was quite a while. And then one afternoon when I had laid down to take a nap because if I got too tired my balance would go and I would fall down a lot. As I lay there, I felt that old seemingly familiar voice feeling and it said come and see. As I lay in bed it seemed to me, I got up and we started out.

This was unlike any dream I had ever had because I could experience feelings that were both in the dream and my memory, which did not work well to begin with. I can only attribute it to what we would call a spiritual vision. Fact but not matter. It seemed like I was going through a tunnel and many things throughout history were flashing by in glimpses. and finally, it stopped and to me it seemed like I was in a quaint country village, yet it had a peaceful feel about it. I was overcome with questions about all that had already happened. I had not been able to interact with the glimpses of history that I had seen while in the tunnel, but I could feel what they were feeling. Now there was such peace.

As I began to listen to the inhabitants. I asked if they could see me, they can see you, you have always been here. It was then I wanted to go to see God. But I listened and all they wanted to do was help each other. They did not seem to judge each other or try to change each other only to help each other. Not just some of them but all of them seeking to help each other. They did not need to ask each other simply they start what they needed help and others would help. I asked and it seemed like they were shocked anyone would ask. Then I was taken to another part or place. It was different because as

I looked back, I saw all of time and space laid out before me kike a paper painting. I heard or felt I could go anywhere I wanted but I waited and was just about floored as I was filled with an energy and joy like I have never seen or felt. And I was shown so many things. I am, told me I am all energy and I will always get greater than you could imagine or conccive all that is of me I will always be greater. All is in me you were in me and are in me and we all are one. We always get greater. In the beginning, all was to get greater because that is what I do in order for the people to do what they choose to make greater.

In order to truly get greater all, have to choose to be part of or not part of the growing process. For that to happen you had to be given the choice. That is why the tree of knowledge between good and evil needed to be in Eden. Because what is good for all, like me always leads to more. Evil is always less than because it is the parts that make the whole. It is always less than what is possible. It too is part of the whole it defines the parts. When I gave men the ability to choose what they would to either grow or reduce the whole I gave them dominion over their individual world, or portion. In order to achieve that they are allowed to choose to be only the part or join the whole. I did this by allowing them to choose what they would feel about, how much they would feel about and why they would feel about anything. In that manner they will judge themselves and receive according to what they chose. The energy that is created is mine the loss of the joy of good feelings is theirs. in that fashion god will always get greater and whoever sets themselves against it always gets lesser. Because it is freely given it will allow them to define or destroy their world. Since it can never be apart from the whole it becomes a part that no one would choose to go. It is by this nature that all was created and therefore it empowers the truth to either encourage or destroy what violates the intent of free will. In that manner, you can see that the destruction of free will eventually leads to the destruction of the groups or individuals that propagate it.

It is true that because you cannot conceive of the whole you will demand to name what you cannot define to have control over all things. In keeping with the freedom to judge only yourself I have caused so many things you could not understand because you think in terms of divided not whole. In keeping with that you need to understand that God does not make mistakes so rather than think about dividing you should think in terms of understanding the whole. it is for this reason most if not all your religions center around the destruction of others. That would indicate that you think God makes mistakes. Rather than understand the intent to raise the joy and energy of life. In the bible it tells of how Lucifer told Adam and Eve that to eat of the tree of knowledge would make them as gods. It would indicate that God did not know what was going on that is typical thinking of man apart from. It was necessary for man to know the truth to freely choose to accomplish the free increase of energy that comes when you raise the joy of living. Therefore, it is part of the plan to give man, the freedom to choose and raise the value. It is the reason one of the commandments is that you shall have no other gods before me. What you choose to give power to has power over you. if you think you can divide or name god you think you are free to do as you will. You can do this by choosing what others say rather than what is, as something you should feel about or that someone else should be able to dictate your feelings even though they cannot feel what you do. The ability to choose what you feel about anything is the freedom to control the feelings of your life. I would

ask you what gods do you have? What really gives

you feelings? Is it money, or the opinions or envy of

others? Is it because someone told you that someone

else interacted with God in a certain fashion? And

if you wanted to interact with the creator of all this

is the only way. It is whatever philosophy you live

by? Most philosophies and stories that survive have

some basis in truth. but the truth is that all are

included not just the ones you recognize. you see

if you think of God as just another powerful man

you indicate he is limited. try to understand how

and why you define something as God. Take care

to understand why you have given something the

power to illicit feelings in you. Is it because someone

or society says you should? The importance of an

individual relationship with your creator is the truth

in finding the freedom he meant for you. why do

you feel what you feel? Is it because you think it is

because it is what you think someone else wants you to feel? The truth will always be the same and if you try to do something that is not because of your feelings of want or your desire eventually you will lose the joy in whatever you have tried to force yourself to accept.

It is this simple understanding of what it is that enables you to see through the eyes of the prophets and children of God that gives you the strength and become a part of not apart from the whole. You see when you find someone, and you both share the joy of that love for each other your joy and energy is so great you feel like you are walking above the ground. It is when you share with someone who feels the same as you. It increases the joy and energy you feel it is it is what you were designed for.

The key to that understanding comes from your vision of who or what god is as he told Moses you could not even conceive of me let alone name me.

I am that I am tell pharaoh I am sent you. You see God is the origin of all energy we divide it into things we can limit to our ability to see. But the truth is that matter is a biproduct of the energy. It is the different forms of energy that created and still shapes matter. We know a little about energy such as solar energy, hydraulic and pneumatic energy because of the results in matter we see. Many think that the creation of energy is caused by the combination of different types of matter. it is the energy in the matter that is infused in the matter that continues. As I said we know a little about energy because it really exists without the time space continuum. Energy transforms it does not go away it is always seeking to increase. Just like God it grows always even though we can't understand. It may change forms, but it does not go away. For instance, solar energy becomes thermal energy then hydraulic energy when it goes from the sun to the ocean. It has different effects at different stages as it works on the things it can work with. So too just because you don't recognize God does not decrease the fact that he is there. It simply will affect the one who does not believe it is evident in their feelings and frustration because it will be present in their lack of joy in life. It is the energy that is attached to matter that even when it is drastically decreased it is still present. That is why deceased animals and plants become fertilizer for new. But as I said all energy is of God, and while we don't understand its many facets or even how to identify it. We think of it in terms of living and dead. But the energy that we are we call our soul it is attached to our matter or body. But like all energy it will seek to grow and find more. But it was because God gave us the choice of deciding what we would feel about and that converts into energy unless it does not join with others to increase the energy. You have the authority to cut yourself off which means you will cease to be recognized or interacted with. Since you will not be able to add more power, you end yourself. For you to understand this in a manner that might help I will use homosexual relationships. The facts are that it takes the energy of a male and a female to produce the energy required for a new creation. the result of the relationship is that their line will be cut off. It is not that they are morally right or wrong it is the fact of creation that physically you have chosen to end your line. Just as if you choose not to seek the continuation of all you end your soul's ability to continue raising the joy for all. It is your spiritual choice to fail to grow that puts you in a place that no one will interact with you. This why Jesus said that we are afraid of the one that can end us physically but do not worry about the one that can end us always. It is not a moral punishment to be homosexual, as all things it is a choice you make for yourself if you choose that it is considered a sin by many because they think in terms of right and wrong by their judgement, after all what Lucifer said is true you can say what you judge things to be in place of God himself. God judged it as missing the mark of taking the gift of life and raising the value to the highest it can be, so he does not allow them to produce an ongoing physical line. It is not our place to judge anyone else the loss of the ability of watching your children grow is what they will have to live with. That I think is enough. So, you see god does not need you to enforce his will it will happen as he planned.

God does not need your help in religion as well he is perfectly capable of rewarding and ending by the nature, he created those religions that violate his will for us to have choice and raise the joy of living which raises the energy of life. In the first place consider what any religion is. One man telling another how someone else supposedly interacted with the creator. When in fact you could not feel what that person felt or, for that matter understand why that person chose to give it power over themselves. You think you want supernatural proof yet when you hear or see it you think it is crazy or rigged. Again, you expect God the creator of all to jump through the hoops for you. It is not that he will not answer but just like your hoops you may not even be open enough to see that answer because it is not what you wanted to hear, or worse yet it is not the way your church limited God. The reason for this book is to tell you that is your individual relationship with the creator of all that that will give you the answers you seek he will do it on an individual basis not to prove himself to whatever social group you have given the authority to establish your feelings, in other words chosen to make your god. Just as in homosexual relationships you are free to choose what you will set up as your god or desire, but eventually the fact that it cannot sustain growth will end it. You can look at the length of its survival and consider the various factions that are under that umbrella and know while there is some truth to what is taught there it is how much truth the individual gives it that will allow it to continue. It is of men not of God it is another way you are given the choice to understand and truly find God within yourself not because someone else said it has to be. At the same time god deals with all in whatever fashion they can understand so you must give them the freedom you expect to have in your search. God is the father of all so it is not one or the other it is how can we live as free brothers?

All of this and so much more I saw in the blink of an eye because as I said I was outside time and in the spiritual world that includes this world but not limited with the start and finish as we are but rather always been and always is. This world is created to give you the freedom to judge yourself and only yourself. It was created so that you by your choices to be unlimited along with God or to have a beginning and an end point. That is true justice, you cannot blame others for what you chose to allow to give you feelings. It seems the world thinks that god will forcefully step in and destroy all who disagrees with them. The reality of it is God will rescue his children as he freed his children by letting them choose and allowing the consequences of those choices to occur. That is also part of the vision what is to be. However, we have not finished with what was and is yet. Because it was told to you long ago in many ways, yet it has occurred it is true and even though you may not like it does not change and you cannot make it go away. Already we have talked so much but there is more to see and know if you are to survive what is yet to be without falling victim to being cut off by your own choice. As you can see in this first chapter there is a story that this spiritual vision gave. One of the things you see right off is that I am telling you of what I saw in heaven, as impossible as that seems I saw heaven and it is not what so many think and yet more than they can imagine a whole world of people who really know "what you do to the least of these you do also unto me." It did not involve money but true value which is the individuals' feelings.

CHAPTER 2

Of Heaven

As I have told you I was in heaven and because I still felt as though I was in physical form it took some time to overcome the shock of this changed world to me. However, the biggest difference was that you did not just hear others you felt their intent. It seemed like the words were just second thought. I was unsure if they felt what I felt, or they were just being different because I was different. I even asked my guide could they see me? His reply was you have always been here they know you. I can't say I really understood but it was enough for me to begin to guess where I had been brought too, so naturally I wanted to see

God. I was expecting some of the imagery it talks about in the Old Testament but what I experienced next was completely overpowering. it was as though I was filled with energy like I had never known, and I understood so many things I had never even considered. All the while this overwhelming sense of peace even though it seemed like even the air was charged with energy. Then as I had begun to come accustomed to that voice that I felt rather than truly heard began to explain and show me how in the beginning I was in him, and the fact was that he is in me, and we were one. I know that this is the reason people refer to Jesus as God because he told them this. And since they cannot understand a god that is truly with them, they did what people do and separated themselves from him and sought to make a deity of him even though when he taught them to pray, he did not start as being apart from but rather with, when he said our father not my father. Further he told them they must be like him reborn to enter heaven. Since we know being physically reborn is not possible to be reborn with a new set of standards and desires that not your will be done but the fathers will be done. How you assign the ability to cause your feelings brand new is to be reborn. To be and see the world as he did is to be like him. Most people say the fact that he died so they are free, have no idea of what gift he truly gave them. And that is why later he himself said in the end many will come to me saying lord, lord. And I will say to them why do you call me lord, but you do not do what I said? So, you see this vision and the visions of so many prophets in so many religions serve the one true god creator of all. And they all talk about his will, but people twist their words to say what they want. The truth does not change that is why so many religions fail because they try to divide rather than serve the whole, they think it gives them power, and to a degree it does. What people give them. What Jesus told them was God loves all of you do not judge or divide his children and he is one with his children. His truth will serve all those who serve the truth, and it does not change.

In heaven all understand that it is to serve all that serves God. his will is the energy of existence, and all are one to divide is to destroy if you come across something that is divided you try to find ways to join it to all or set it apart never to be sought. Not because you judged it that way because it judges itself that way by seeking to be apart. It is true always in order to have the energy that will sustain existence you need to not separate yourself. It is truly peace that does not contend with anything or anybody. It is amazing in that there are no borders yet there is separation from all that will be separate. Yet I can see because it is free choice given by our father it can be. i see and I know I can feel that it is in keeping with the will of the father. There seems to be so many wonders that are almost indescribable. The lack of borders is amazing. Again, I was overwhelmed by the presence of peace and our father and as I looked out, I saw everything laid out before me. it seemed like there were so many rooms and yet they were all one not contending with one another, and I understood something else Jesus said my father's house has many rooms, I go to prepare one for you and if I go, I will surely come back for you.

While there are many rooms in my father's house it is not because there is no desire for separation, all are gods' children and the feelings that you had the freedom to choose, is the ultimate value. In fact, it is the only definition of value. Consequently, it does not matter what room you are in just that you are in the father's house. While there are differences in the appearance and gifts the inhabitants have the reality is that it is how we all not only are one, but we apply all our gifts to help advance all. it is not our differences that count but how we use them to raise the joy of all. Many here will not be able to understand but what will be. remember it is not the individual alone that can raise value it requires two or more to feel the same way and share that with each other. Since you are not tied to time you do not have to worry about age. Most will appear as they did when they were the absolute happiest here, because they are as close to the one when they were like that. As a result of the fact that some only had a short time to experience that state here, before their time here was done. This too is why Jesus said suffer the little children to come to me for of such is the kingdom of heaven.

It could take a million words to describe heaven but the words that best describe it are peace and joy undivided, they would not consider judging one another but hold and expect all to hold them as themselves. For as surely as you do unto the least of these you do also unto me.

CHAPTER 3

Of Earth

The first days of earth were given to those who had chosen the knowledge of good and evil. They were filled with new sensations that they never really needed or have in heaven. The main over all feeling was that of being isolated. It was so alien that it made them seek to isolate themselves further. So much so that when our father came near, he knew they had separated themselves. The bible says they realized they were naked, since naked was not even known then it is the first reference to sex. As a result of that association sex became entangled with people's perception of the original sin. Because of the immediate association of sex with being separate everyone new that sex and the feeling assigned to it could make the other person experience shame. It became one of the primary control mechanisms that people used to control one another. It was a personal display of weakness that no other creature demonstrated. What it taught them was that while you could not directly control one another's feelings in a natural state, you could have your feelings manipulated. The initial concept of society relied on this to control conduct in the group. For this to work you had to convince the individual the group new more than the individual about feelings. If this manipulation worked how about the value of what something means or should mean? This is the belief that society relied on to establish economic and monetary scales how much your feeling should be worth. The fact that God gave the individual the right to determine what they would feel about and why by doing this he gave you dominion of your own world only. In heaven the individual was never disconnected from the whole in this world that truth they thought they could change. The reason for that goes back to Lucifer telling them that the knowledge would make you feel like God, what he did not tell you is that because God gave you the right to choose, others can also choose what they want.

Consequently, people thought of themselves as God and that meant what was important to them should be important to all. In order to get what they wanted they had to control what others felt. The way to do this has all to do with, how and what people decide what they will feel about and why. This is possible by fear and force. Either to convince them that someone ese knows better than you or killing those who chose something else. as a result when someone talked ab0ut God their response was to kill those who did not understand him the same way they did. That is why in the Old Testament and many of the oldest scriptures the people were supposedly told to kill everyone and everything. This type of doctrine furthered the division and isolation of individuals and groups as well. They justified this by saying you would receive the worth of those people you had removed. Again, the concept of worth being and maintained by something else besides yourself. Because it works to a point more and more people bought into the concept. It continued again and again and gradually expanding the depth of control others exercise over each other it continues to this day and is a repetitive process. The fact that in groups your ability to defend yourself and others increases is the truth they used to produce the fear of being unable to defend yourself or accepting the right for society to determine what and how much you should feel. It is the kernel of truth in their lie. That is why it is demonstrated repeatedly the miraculous exceptions. To the point that people gave their sons and daughters to be killed in the attempt to give the leadership of their social group's desires. It continues today and it continues to remove true value from your lives, it increases still the isolation. It is this underlying lie that has brought the world to the brink of self-destruction. The fact that God gave the feelings of good when you are involved sexually physical nerve cause you to feel good. But to society they had to make you overcome those feelings and allow them to tell you what you should feel. That is, it becomes important to enforce their concept. The reality of the fact that love does not operate by property right laws. Makes this control evidently false without threat to enforce the property law aspects, because this is a lie we have deteriorated as a society. Up to and practically through the destruction of the nuclear family. Therefore, you see the many lies we give authority over our lives by allowing the concept that others know more or have the power to establish our feelings, do not change the fact that you have control only of your own feelings and life.

I hope you will take the time to see how the prophets tried to tell you and show you the same thing. And in seeing what they said instead of what someone else said about them or said they said you can find the truth. When you find the truth no matter what time in history or whatever situation you look at it never changes, the truth does not change. There are many prophets from different religious back grounds, but the truth does not change, so you need to see that they are just a relevant today as they were in their time. This understanding will help you to see what was said will happen if you seek the truth know that while the things they talked about or tried to explain was and is contained in understanding. That is why most people can't even describe what heaven should be like. It is also the reason that society is being torn apart by people who promote lies. Statements about someone hurting your feelings, when you obviously didn't care about theirs. Promoting the policies that have only one end in destruction giving authority to lies as though they were truth. I will talk a great deal about one prophet in particular, Jesus, because he told you the truth in a way that others had to hide because they did not see or understand what he was telling them. Therefore, he is the messiah because he told the truth. We talk about how he died for us, but he talked about how he lived for them. People chose to deify him separately even though he never said to. He said to deify our father who is in all. he said in the beginning I was in my father, my father is in me, we are one. This is what the lie cannot allow because it takes away the authority, they try to convince you they have over you. Again, the doctrine of men is to be apart from God. Because they can demand that what they say is the truth. All is contained it is when you try to concentrate on the parts without trying to improve all you throw away what you do not include.

People would say what they do not understand is not real, and they cannot understand the things Jesus said. I am going to point out to you that Jesus told his followers that because of him father against son mother against daughter, brother against brother. Because he saw what was going to come. He saw what they could not see. The churches and Christian religion like all religion is controlled by men and teaches what men want to hear because of their perceived economic and power structure again based on what they could control as value. He told them what was going to happen, in fact it went like this, "who do people say I am? you think I came to give you peace I have given you a sword. It was his vision of the thousands of tears about to happen around the context and failure to understand we are one. Again, it is about power men want to be the ones who say who will have power. It is important that you understand this because it reinforces the prediction of a thousand years before Jesus. This prophecy also talked of two witness and what was to be. the first part was done with Jesus, so I would say the second part is as assured to come as well. In fact, many have taken the liberty to say how that comes to be. they talk of armies from heaven lead by Jesus to destroy those who stood against the church's teachings. Even though he refused to condemn even the ones who hung him. They have him coming back to judge us. After all the teaching he did over not judging others, they cast him as a judge. At best they cast him as a defense attorney. Who paid so we could miss behave? They say that all you must do is say his name, when he said in the end many will come to me saying" lord, lord." And "I will say to them why do you call me lord when you do not do what I said." You must try to be as he is and as he was. It is not worth nothing it is to discover the true father. All the things I talk about here is what he said. We watch movies and think of people who stood for what they believed even up to death. We think of them as heroes, if they lost their lives in what we consider valuable. It is easiest when it is society that supports this. However, today religions and truth are ridiculed. All form the constant process of reducing the only true value with the value of society, or I would say the mob.

It is the entire process of how you decide value or worth that is the question. They want to maintain value as a mysterious quality that only they can decide. If it be in spiritual or material, it is theirs to control. This has caused millions of people to die. They rely on you teaching your children that they know better. As a result, your sons and daughters die at someone else request. Then they wonder why it only leads to more atrocities. Still, they try to ask it a moral question because they don't think you can supply truth or question them with fact. Unfortunately, people still offer their sons and daughters lives to people who believe they are entitled to demand the death of our children. They don't think they are one of the people they think they are better than the people and despite the deaths we allow it. There are times when we are and should be committed to helping protect our neighbors, if they ask for and try to defend themselves. It should not be done on a limited basis because our children's lives are at stake. To begin with the concept of killing them all is the way war should be conducted. That way people will stop playing games with life. It should horrify all who seek to enter war. That is the

way it will stop. We are one and the only way to be
one is to live as one. Do not judge each other but
hold each accountable to how they judge themselves
by what they say and do. This is what true mercy
means it is the only thing Jesus told the Sanhedrin
he requires. No political figure should be reelected
if they are responsible for the death of our children
by failing to provide the proper support to those,
they send in harm's way. To enter a war zone in less
than full force is to play with war and all it does is
keep the failed leadership in charge. If you commit
to help do all you can to protect and help or your
commitment means nothing. I know people will
react in horror at such a suggestion but World War
three will happen as a result of the failure of people
to understand true value and allowing the loss of all
the freedoms god gave you. It will just seem to take
longer until one side or the other uses weapons of
mass destruction. I know what is coming and that is

yet to be told what I have talked about to this time has and is happening now.

Destroy this temple and I will rebuild it in three days. That is what Jesus told the Jewish church leadership. It sounds unbelievable today, just as it did then. What do you think your reaction to that would be if a trial was covered on tv today and the defendant said such a thing? Is there any wonder why you say Jesus next return will be at the head of an army? Have you ever considered that God hid Jesus from Herod despite the prophets telling him what was going to happen, until he had done what he was sent to do? Are you so convinced that God wants to kill you that the only saving grace is a war? and what do you think the ground rules for such a war only people from a certain portion of a certain religion are left alive and only the dead of that religion will be raised? Or do they do as the Old Testament says and kill them all? Or is it liking the scriptures say and the second witness just like the first is killed and then raised in three days. I know it says that there will be an army from heaven and the dead will be raised to join that army, but consider what god would feel with the destruction of so many of his children? More importantly how would God grow from that? I am suggesting that you will think about what you have been taught and how you have given it the power over you. Because that is how you will be judged by yourself. Are you free as Jesus was? Can you hang on the cross based on what your church taught you? If you did, could you forgive those who hung you, or even remember they were just doing their job? Could you hang there and talk to God? Would you have even gone knowing what was about to happen? As I have told you from his own words and mouth he knew. I know there have been other prophets that talked about what has been and even what will be in many different religions even those that have been to heaven to see God. How many came back telling you God wants you all to die? Or to go out and kill anyone who does not agree with you? If they did, they would not be around long. As clearly, I have stated their followers may say that they did but that is not in any way serving anyone or God. I have told you to check for yourself ask our father he wants to hear from you if you call yourself a Christian do as he told you and even from the cross talk to the father. if you are not a Christian or you do not know have the guts to talk to God as your father and see how he answers you it may take some getting used too we don't even do a good job of listening to each other. I am sorry if you do not feel you can talk to God or if you feel others have to or should talk to him for you. You might struggle thinking what language trust me just like this vision I am writing to you about no language necessary.

I guess as I have been trying to show you the past and the present are tied together so is the future, so I need to start with now. I hope you will forgive me it has been over a year since I sat down and listened to any news coverage for more time than it takes to change the channel or turn it off. I rely on understanding why and what will happen. It is not that difficult if you understand true value and the means men use to create the value, they want you to believe. The reason I have done this is the same understanding what others say are indications of how they judge themselves, since the prevailing sentiment is to allow others to dictate to you what they want you to believe. In short, the news used to just be reported and it was allowed to judge itself by the results of what it created. People were free to decide for themselves what it represents. Today the news is a tirade of politically motivated policy. And it is spun for that effect. It is accomplished again by value, or social value which is money. Again, the reporters sell their integrity for political approval. This lack of standing for what you believe is fueling the loss of social value. It is further reinforcing the fear to stand up for your belief. It used to be you might have suffered some verbal insult and harm, today it could easily be physical harm. If they can brazenly do this in front of the entire public and suffer no consequences, they can certainly be bought. This is an indicator of how far the progression of loss of true value has advanced. It is also an indicator of the state of the people that they would allow it to go this far. Again, the loss of faith which can be demonstrated is the result of the failure of religions to demonstrate the relevant truth. Teaching a partial truth is just setting it up for total rejection. That is why today so many say that God is a concept that is not real. Again, the result of not being able to point to the causative failures in a world that has advanced to the point what you say now can be on the other side of the earth in seconds. when most of the scriptures were written it may have taken years or decades to get out of the continent they were written on. With the increase of the speed of communication so also the loss of true value because people do not understand the nature of true value which is what enables others to replace what you value with what they value, and use it to belittle and reduce your understanding, but all that really happens is that you feel depressed and less than what you should have felt which is empowered. It is your willingness to accept what others say in place of what you see is that loss of value that they rely on because you feel the loss but do not understand it they tell you your faith is misplaced. Because you accepted their words over your feelings your faith is misplaced. They want to talk about me when in reality me is we, you lose the ability to raise the joy and value of life with everyone you cut out of your life, and to cut someone out because someone else told you too without seeing with your own eyes, and directly from that person prevents you from finding ways to find the, we, and the me is really the society rather than you. It really is summed up in some simple old-time wisdom, if someone tells you to jump off a cliff would you, do it? Is just as true if you accept someone else's statement that God does not exist. Their understanding of God is faulty. They envision themselves as God and want to demand that everything is as they say. Instead of true value which is their feelings that only them can feel. You see God himself gave you the authority to decide what and how much you will feel is yours. In that way you establish what you value. If you understand that then you understand true individual value. It is reinforced by what is real. And when you find someone who genuinely feels as you do those feelings

are magnified and intensified, it is the only true way
to increase the value of your feelings and it is this
process to raise the joy of living that is the reason
you were given this time and place. Raising the
value of creation is what it was created for. It always
leads to more it is good. What is evil losing value
always. as simple as it is, it is the one knowledge
that empowers creation itself. It is the one teaching
that Jesus kept trying to make clear to you, it is this
that he gave to you because of this you can truly
see why he is the savior. Yet all those around sought
to turn his words to what they felt and since people
seek what they knew death became the gift he gave
not the freedom of value. Look at the world around
you. There are people who say there is no god. And
it is being given authority socially. Socialism which
is all about supposedly the distribution of value
according to someone else scale. A political system
that can only work by the stealing of the individuals

value and because of that fault it contains its own destruction. Which is why it can never succeed. While people cannot define things, they deny the existence of them. People seek lies as though they are the truth. There are wars and rumors of wars there are smart disease and pandemics. It seems I have heard that before yes, it is in the bible and even though this thing was written about three thousand years ago, it has to be a modern hoax according to new stream thinking.

Let us consider some of the other social things going on now in the world. Racism, it is unfortunate that it ever existed, but it has existed as long as men have been in any social form. The difference is that today we hold the grandchildren accountable for what their grandparents did. It doesn't matter that in most cases the ones that sold others into slavery were the same race and there are and have been probably slaves of every race and ethnicity, but we will select one race to blame for this. We won't hold those grandchildren of the ones who sold their brethren into slavery or the ones of the same race that bought their brethren and sold them to another race. We really don't have accurate figures, but we still have places in the world white, Latino, Asian, and blacks, are still enslaved but we want to hold the people of one of the countries that will not allow slavery responsible for the system. We don't consider the fact that for socialism to come to power in China the death of forty million people, in the Soviet Union twenty million people disappeared, but there is no injustice according to the social mainstream because they are socialist. The fact that system can only exist if it has people to steal from and an elite portion of people to decide who gets what. It seems while they seek and promote this system as a social goal despite the facts that until a country that has the military force, and the concentration type camps to have dissenters disappear into it is a stylish lie that people are not protesting. So amazing how that someone thousands of years ago would see that coming. By the way all those things were written about the end of the world as we know it. Or the end of days. How they could have seen all of this is impossible and it must be a plot. The truth is being denied daily. So, you see the future is also rooted in the past what I have said are what Jesus said I have detailed why and how you can see for yourself. They point out how and why all of this is logical and can be apparent for you. It has all been before you for thousands of years, yet it has not been taught. A different way of seeing things or a new perspective. Yet it requires all that has happened in order to see it. Yet they knew it was coming thousands of years ago. It is what is happening today without stretching or trying to make what was said fit what is going on. This is important to see in order to see what is still to come. As crazy as it may sound it is how exact the match between what was said and what is. I know that people have been trying for years to make what has been foretold to the world they live in. like most things if you think you must manipulate things to make them fit it is probably not true. What I have told you to this point is something that you can check and see for yourself. What I am about to tell you. Is something that I hope you will understand and see for yourself. In order to see and know what is in the future you must see what has been, which is what I have told in this book. As well as other people telling the same story when there is no way to collaborate. What you choose to believe must come from within. People are so used to thinking someone can force someone else to see, but I promise you this if you think God will force you or anyone to change to be in heaven you will never see heaven. No force is any part of heaven it is his mercy that requires you to empower what you will and then you will receive it and that is also what is going to happen here. Whether you believe what I will say here or not does not change the truth of what will be. everyone wants to know the hour and minute, yet if they worry about time, they will never see heaven, it is a choice not forced. The whole point of this book is finding and raising the value of life to be in heaven that is how you and everyone who will be there to choose and live. If you think anyone needs changed by an outside source, you or they will not be in heaven. It is almost impossible for people who claim to have faith to think that heaven can occur on earth yet that is also told what is coming. How much faith do you have, how limited by your judgement are you?

I ask you to consider the state of the world in complete detail, what do you think the world values? What do you think the people have faith in? how do you think most people expect the end of the world as we know it. How many people seem open to understanding anything given that most people do a terrible job of listening to themselves or to each other. So how many do you think are willing to listen to what so many think does not exist?

You may not like it or agree with it but what you are about to hear will happen. You may not recognize the transition in the seemingly small steps, but they will occur rapidly. Because so many are expecting intervention, they may not see the change in the individual but that is where the change will be. because and connected to the judgement day. It has begun and people will judge themselves. What I will tell you is how it can affect or protect you. Just as I have shown you, the truth that was written so long ago has not changed. Why do you think the ending will? That ending is of heaven here on earth. This is an intervention it does not require force. It requires you to control your own actions and choose to not participate in the lies anymore. It requires you to teach the whole truth, even though you will offend people who don't know the father. Or choose a different name for him or description because in that way they think they can control him. Or decide what he will give them. You must be as Jesus was able to not change or apologize and be faith full when you are you will not know the second death which comes when you turn your back on increasing the joy of living. You will be separated and alone forever.

CHAPTER 4

The Start Of A New Time

Up to this point I have told you what I had seen and why it was shown me. It will continue with what I saw because it is the basis to answer the one thing Jesus said in his defense to the Jewish church leadership Roman leader everything this book is about was so that you could answer this. "I require mercy, I do not require sacrifice, if you knew the difference, you would know where my authority comes from." this is what he said when they sought to find out how he performed what they considered miracles. While they thought to convict him, they were in fact beginning the conviction of all. Because in order to answer that you must know who gave him the authority which is God. The father whom he served even unto death. In order to do that you have to know God as your father. If you do, pick up your cross and follow me. that question has waited to be answered for two thousand plus years. Contained in these pages are the answer in order to see it you must know the answer to the original sin and why it was a sin. Which means you need to know him well enough to understand why all this was necessary. If you know that, you can see what the answer to that question is, to know God as your father, which means you have become as Jesus was, one with the father in the beginning, the father is in you now, and you are one. that is what you will need to know in your heart to survive what will come next. The reason for that is that even though many will try to convict you according to their will. But like Jesus you will serve the father

and like Jesus you will have life more abundantly.
You see dying is not living if you die you are cut off
but living requires the ability to take the gift God
the father gave you and make it worth more, that
is what mercy does, taking something of value and
wasting it or throwing it away is sacrifice. That is
what men do not understand they try to say they
are the same thing, but they are not because it is
a value statement not a material statement. One
can raise the joy for all who understand the other
is just a waste of joy. And since joy is energy, one
is a waste or loss of energy the other increases and
makes it greater which is what good does. It is
the purpose of this creation. in short God always
increases, as does good. Evil and sacrifices and
removes value and energy. I pray that you will
understand this have the ears to hear it the eyes to
see it and the heart to know it. Because once you do
you can know our father in a way they cannot take

away. All of this is needed to survive judgement day, which people will bring on themselves. It is what they have always done.

It is this understanding or lack of understanding that results in the largest failure in our churches and religions today. Because of not addressing the needs nor only from a physical standpoint but an emotional spiritual as well we have lost entire generations. That is what you see in the world today. I talk to people who think in terms of physical needs as their definition of love. They really do not connect the spiritual or sometimes even the emotional aspect as part of their definition of love and if you try to draw it out of them they have no clue what you are searching for. It is this thing we have taught that judgement rather than love allows them to judge rather than sit back and observe how things judge themselves that has brought us to this point. Having had a brain injury I thought I had lost so much but the radical change in perception cleared my vision to what is truly important. It is just another obstacle, what you do with it will determine what quality of life you will have. Not what others say but finding a group that while they deal with their own obstacles encourage and help you live what you have the best way you can which requires that you may need to find new ways to find joy in your life. Instead, many fall into the trap of going to places and end up being depressed rather than motivated. Understand loss of emotional value is perhaps more traumatic than physical value. Your obstacles are there to help you find strength that you will need in your walk.

Consider yourself as the parent of a child that refuses to accept anything you try to give them. In order to address that situation, you may need to shock them into reality. Now consider if you waited till, they pushed to the point you had no other option. You love them and know the misery they are bringing on themselves, but you can only wait till they prove it to themselves to help. That is the stage the world has entered. You have been fore warned repeatedly but you refuse change. Because you don't feel you have to. Now the world is expecting that someone will force them to change. The reality of heaven is that all must individually choose that life to experience it and it is not something that someone else can give them or force upon them, because then it would not be heaven. It is about the raising of joy therefore the only ones who can participate in it have to have their own joy to begin with and then sharing it with someone else who knows that and feels that will raise that joy exponentially. That is what heaven is. Because we are linked in the physical time space dimension, we have difficulty accepting that the spiritual emotional side be considered. Even though if you think about it everything we have begun as a thought or mental energy that our bodies made a physical reality. People try to ignore that fact. because they cannot materially identify that energy process. So, it must not be real to a growing portion of our world this is what is happening. Now think are we at the stage that only allowing us to receive what we have set ourselves up for is the shock the world needs. We now have weapons that can kill off most of the population of earth immediately and eventually we think all the rest soon. We are thinking to carry this judgement virus into space. We want to find the other rooms in our father's house so we can plunder them in order to keep feeding our lie. I would say it is time physically for what has existed emotionally and spiritually we call it judgement day. The difference again comes to value. And what will lead to more. The scriptures tell us that heaven will exist on earth. The truth demands that increase occurs, what is going to happen must include all to be whole. The good and the bad must be sorted out but how does that happen according to men war and force are necessary. More destruction.

What will happen is rooted in what has happened and it is already starting. The inability to talk with one another because of the political social pressure will increase. In order to maintain what they perceive as power the leadership of nations will continue entering wars, and because people are too afraid to stand up many of our sons and daughters will die because of their greed for power and the ability to steal the value of a people. They think that force is an answer, if people allow this it will not change, is what they think. So, if I keep them afraid to stand up then I can continue to maintain power. So how do I do that? War has always been a means of diverting attention and the leaders' children are in a safe place. We will destroy any attempt to solidify the people. If they can paint the people as outsiders who are violent and seek to destroy the status quo they can invoke a social morality that is really neither true social nor moral. But this is how the change begins people begin to look for the true father of all and they see in his creation an answer. Be as water absorb flow around do not resist but sweep away gradually. What that means is individually turn your back to the leadership and the media they have attained power over. Do not financially buy anything that supports them. Do not agitate but as you deal with your neighbor allow them to judge themselves by what they say and do. Hold them accountable to that by not allowing their feeling to corrupt or sway, you absorb it but do not rise to it. This will teach you how they judge themselves and who you can reasonably trust. When you gather any time leadership that tries to divide the people, appear turn your back to them. When the news comes on turn your back to them do not financially support anything or anyone whose money empowers the stranglehold on the people. If they send a police line which they will be as water do not resist flow around do not institute violence it will destroy you. Also do not allow any one among you to commit violence against those sent to supposedly restore peace and order. There should be no violence protest by not engaging. Detain anyone who engages in violence and turn them over. If you do this there will be no disorder or need for the police to restore any order. The same is true for the police or any political protective detail. You do not need to look your charge in the face turn your back on them after all the threat to them is that person in the crowd that is trying to incite violence. The same is true for the military all branches and ranks, an illegal order is one that would have you fire on a peaceful crowd. Especially if that crowd refuses to mask those people who seek death. Understand that no matter what country you live in or are from the people they are telling you to fire on are your brothers and the children of god who are not engaging in violence if you fire on them your leaders are seeking to make you murderers. Because they have been successful at this in the past people do not trust you. In order to gain that trust back you need to show yourself worthy of trust. I do not tell you not to protect the people but to remember the people are all the children of god and they will judge themselves by what they do it is equally important that the police and the crowd isolate and prosecute all those who judge themselves worthy of receiving what they sought for others. If you want to be in heaven live like you are and it will come to you. Parents teach your children this and tell them to observe the water it gives and eventually covers all things that it is sent to cover.

The true point of this is that people will begin to listen again to what they are really saying to each other. And they will again learn to share again with each other. At first it will seem like secretly because until you learn to listen to each other you do not trust each other this is because you think you can judge each other. But as this learning process begins and goes on you get better at seeing how all things judge themselves and by watching we can learn what trust is. you think you can fool each other but the father is with all of the time, and he can and will magnify the feelings you give yourself by this judgement process. This is the reality of true justice it does not come from without, just as true corruption comes from within. Jesus again told you and demonstrated this, when walking in the fields he plucked and ate fruit that had not been blessed and when con fronted about it he simply pointed out, "it is not that which enters you that corrupts you but rather that, which comes from you." Again, the wisdom of truth. People will finally embrace that wisdom and not let violence corrupt them and not provide cover for those who commit violence for that two Is something that comes from within and corrupts you. If we begin to hold these truths true and live accordingly it will create heaven here. But because it takes everyone needs to be part of heaven to exist for anyone everyone must hold each other accountable to how they judge themselves and any failure in small things to do this will lead to failure in bigger things. The true purpose of punishment is to raise the value of the life they could choose to share. As we go on, we find that our leaders have less freedom to wantonly send our sons and daughters to die for their ego and lust. People will look at who they are voting for and how they judge themselves by what they vote for. It will not be by political party or the will of others it will be based on how the candidates judge themselves by what they stand for. The concept of force needing to be employed to accomplish will be unthinkable.

The true nature of social is that everyone willingly works to improve the joy of life for each other and themselves. People stop judging what someone else has but sees how they use what they have to improve the joy for as many as they can. At the same time this requires that they do not squander the gifts they have been given but make the value grow by using it in a manner that helps as many as possible. It is not for someone else who does not have those gifts to judge someone who has. God is ever getting greater the universe as we know it is always getting grater at an astounding rate we can see this but our greed prevents us from seeing how even the gifted use their gifts to improve the energy of life itself. But it is because they don't do it the way we think they should we judge them poorly. Did we ever stop to think that if they did what we think they would not have what we do not have?

These realizations will become apparent to those

who really seek to be in heaven. Their children will be raised in the truth they will not be blinded by social manipulation. Their children that are in law enforcement will refuse to fire on their family. Their children who are in the military will refuse to use weapons against those who demand that their government stop trying to determine what their value is or should be. they will turn their backs and refuse to follow an illegal order. They will refuse to be divided by society. By race economic status or by the opinions of others they will understand that like everything else all value starts within and if they are to have heaven it must come from within all of the individuals and that knowledge coupled with the fact that they are not judging simply holding each other accountable to how they judge themselves, they will have the strength necessary to live in heaven.

Therefore, you see why heaven will and must exist here, as it was told to you thousands of years ago but it is your judgement of each other that prevents it. So let us consider some of the other things you were told from the same source. Most of which because they are subject to men who wants it to say what they want it to say based on their understanding. So, when it was foretold of the coming messiah, it included things that they certainly could not understand. It talks of two witnesses it promised a savior and as usual they took that to be in this physical world for them now. It was a thousand years before it was fulfilled, in fact because it did not deliver politically many questioned if it had been fulfilled at all. It is again something that so many do not really give too much thought to. But it is the full prophecy that would come true few today understand the importance of what it said. It foretold the coming and the death of the one who would come. it also foretold the raising of the witness after they had killed him. Because it ended in death it was discounted as far as what delivery it brought the first part of the prophecy has happened. But what of the rest of the prophecy about the second witness who would meet the same fate as the first? It is something that the religious leaders cannot explain. Yet, just as the first part was true the second will also occur. But like all things that are true it does not change, as much as people try to change it. But, as with the rest of the prophet's direction it does not stand alone but is coupled with further prophecy sometime centuries later. It is the ongoing unchanging truth that becomes self-evident. if you understand then you will see that the second coming does not change what the first coming did and stood for. the reception will be the same because the truth does not change neither does the centuries old misunderstanding. In short, I believe love is always raising the joy of life, it is not and should never have been a questu9n of property rights. Your only true value comes from the joy of your feelings, so if you do not have joy you need to look at your definition of love. In keeping with the combination of prophecy and truth the first witness gave you a sword that you tried to turn on each other, the second will lose that sword to do what it was created to do. Turn on those who refuse to dedicate themselves to the raising of the gift of life through the sharing with others that raises the joy for all. Because people have not changed, they will kill the second witness as well. The difference is the first was here to tell you the truth and show you its truth the second is come to tell you the truth has not changed. And it is still the choice of the individual only to find and love the father and be one with the father. Just as Jesus told them to. Jesus needed his group to establish his continued teaching after they had killed him. He knew he would not be ended but his death was to provide the truth to challenge each individual and in those days there was no internet and it could take much more than a lifetime to get the truth throughout the world. The second witness is in a time of practically instant communication worldwide. He is not here to establish a new religion but to point out the truth of the father no matter how you individually think you can define him. He is not here to judge you. Each will do that yourself as always it will still take time for those established structures of social custom to realize they have been told the same truth and it has not changed in spite of the ways they claimed it would. Since he has not come to create a new truth, his death is not to buy the individual's time. This time his death will lose the sword Jesus gave to be turned on those who seek to divide and destroy the children of God. It will be the combination of judgement day and the destruction which so many people expect to come but to who they want to divide and destroy. Between the people who understand and become as the water which will help preserve them even as they stand for truth. But because many have never known what true love is. And many seek to judge others as a matter of routine, they won't even seek to see or understand the truth. This continuation without resistance like water will speed up their destruction of themselves. This will cause more to consider what both witnesses actually said that consideration will enable more people to know the truth, and once they know the truth will realize that to divide or judge others will only speed up their own destruction. As the truth becomes even more evident it will grow not by force but by reward in the individual's joy. That cannot be done by anyone else. More will know a one on one relationship with the father of all. The second witness will raise just as the first did but the established social institutions we call the church will do whatever they can to hide or deny what is. This also has been foretold thousands of years ago. But it is not in keeping with those who seek to remain divided from god. They think of fear of our father is to be a staff to beat the children with. So, understand what each was to do. The way most people think of this time in the history of man that Jesus comes with an army to force and kill man. But reality is Jesus was hidden from Herod and until he did what he was sent to do most did not even know him. The same will occur with the second he will be hidden and just as before it will be after they do what it is said they will do that the sword will be loosed to turn on those who would turn it on others. At this point the death of those who convict themselves will accelerate through all manner of things they themselves have empowered. Again, they will attempt to distract but this time all it will do is destroy them quicker. Even this is used to help others understand the reality of the truth. In all this devastation and destruction, they will finally admit that true value is with what you feel and why, it is not dependent on 0ther people it does not change, it is this being between a rock, which is what people think of their will as, and a hard place which is the truth that will not change, which will increase the number who will know the truth. This process will take a while but, in the end, will reveal everyone's state.

Now I need to point out again the fact that Jesus said he would come back. Along with the prophecies of old it is a fact that he will but how well did you understand him? I and my father are one, why do you call me lord when you do not do what I said. Pick up your cross and follow me. All are Jesus and all are the fathers. So who ever he sends will have the same understanding, they will also know as Jesus did what is going to happen and just like Jesus he knows they will kill him and yet he knows also that he serves the father unto death and beyond.

Again, the difference is it is up to you if you will be saved because it is up to you to understand can the son of man forgive sin? He has come to confirm it is time you must judge yourself and you will be held accountable now. Between the arrival of the second witness the first has returned, the judgement is being enforced those who have judged them apart from God will lose all ability to interact with that which is of God. What does that mean again I point to thousand-year-old scripture. What burns but does not consume? The answer is the energy of your will.

It is this burning that they have condemned themselves to forever since in order to increase joy they have to share it. Yet, they have cut themselves off from all that is good. Hell, as promised burns and cannot be extinguished. How many of you have felt the burning sensation of your desires but were not consumed?

Therefore, what has been foretold has become

fulfilled and if you are to be there heaven will be on earth and so much more will be opened to you. As you become more intertwined knowledgeably with the creator of all you will find what used to seem like bonds do not restrict you as they did when you were apart from. But your joy does not make you want to see more because it would divide and that is what put everyone through this to begin with. And dividing is not something you would ever want. The things in heaven are not locked like here because they are not limited as you become more one with the father the authority over things increases so you refuse disease and age because the father and you are no longer chained to time or space. We cannot comprehend that now but it is promised and demonstrated again in scripture that are thousands of years old.

As I have tried to do from the start of this book is to tell you that who i am is not important, I would say I am the least of those who serves our father. But I will always do my best to serve and help raise the joy in the gift of life that he gave us. I am in him as well so what he said is still true as surely as you do onto the least of these you do also onto me. Since the energy of life is the gift, he gave us and the ability to increase the energy of life by raising the joy of life. That is what you were created for and it increases the source of all energy our father god. Most people want this portion to continue and are so consumed with a portion I hope you want to make it greater.

I know you think the story of man and creation should be so much longer and if I wanted to divide everything to tell you what I thought you should believe, but as I have repeatedly said it is not what I know or say to you that will save you for you have been given the truth if you chose to know and do what you were shown you can save yourself. I can tell you that what you want to know will be given ask the father but don't make up your mind what the answer must be, learn to listen.

CHAPTER 5

What's Your Vision

People who read this arc looking at my vision and trying to see through my eyes what I saw. However, unless they could see the multitude of things that flashed through my mind, they would not be able to see what I did and conclude what I saw because the truth does not change. So, they would ask themselves what this means for me, if they are wise. The reality of vision is not that you can make others see what you did but open them to make their own conclusions and choices in their life. Many think the vision is what you want to decide to see, but the truth is you will see a whole lot of things you wish you had never seen. That is why Jesus said more blessed is he who believes but does not see.

As an example, imagine if you will how he saw how his words and teachings would be twisted and turned so that others would deify him even though he never said pray to me but he did say pray with me. That is why he told his disciples because of my mother against daughter, father against son, brother against brother. It is not what he taught but the words were twisted so people could justify that, and the church teaches that. Because they presume to point to the name of Jesus as the only way to be saved, the reality is the teachings of his word in the right and full disclosure so you can live as he showed you is the salvation he brought. The vision you think is joy but many times it is pain to see what people will do and misuse each other because of their definition of what was said. That is why you were told no man knows the hour or the day of judgement. Because you are dealing with something that is not physical or controlled by time it does not exist for all, it like your faith and God always is your moment is your choice. What many are waiting for is the force being used to destroy what they don't like. In doing this they seek control not God, so they have to put it in context to what they know which is day and hour. It is this failure of allowing each to make decisions for themselves that they think gives them the right to say who goes to heaven and what god can and cannot do. So, let us talk vision in reality no ones vision will prevent your death, you were born you will die at least physically. The question for vision is will you die at peace no matter when it is your time? That depends on what you choose to believe and give power over yourself too. If you are divided, you will not have peace. If you are filled with vengeance, you will not have peace, if you put yourself above God because you think you have the right to decide for others you will not have peace. As I have said it is not how things apart are but, the reality of how they fit together so all is and is used to raise the joy and energy of the gift that you have which is the energy that is life, that will give you peace. My vision is filled with a lot of things I would not wish others to see coming, but they will still come not because our father wants them too but because the children chose them too and empowered them so they could inflict misery on anyone who does not see things as they do. It is this part of the vision that makes you wish you never saw it. At the same time what you see you know is real. And because you know it is you can still have peace because it is the freedom for each to choose for themselves that although people want to take that freedom away the only way they can is through force, or you are giving it to them. which is what they use the force for. If you do not, they cannot take it, they may kill your physical form but not you. And because the weakness that comes with being tied to time goes away you will be greater than they could imagine and by doing what they did they have sought for themselves the burning sensation of loneliness and misery for eternity because they have removed the ability to share and grow the joy of the gift they had but through away.

Perhaps because this seems so philosophical, we need to look at it through the eye of the **here and now.** As I have said, I had a traumatic brain injury and except for anyone who has truly suffered one no one can appreciate all of the levels of your life that is affected by one. Our best medical and psychological doctors are barely scratching the surface of trying to deal with the myriad of symptoms that are a result. The treatments and recovery range from barbaric to bizarre. They try to portray themselves as professional which in many cases they are however if it were a mechanical issue, they can be extremely knowledgeable and, in many cases, capable of dealing with the deficits. Because they are attempting to deal with psychological feelings they fail miserably and, in many cases, damage the patients in a way that will slow or even prohibit their recovery. Of course, they would deny this or point out it is not an exact science. They are trying to do their best in a world that is not black and white but many shades. It took almost two years for a doctor to even recommend a support group that does not seem as important such as humor, people begin to look forward to sharing not in a negative way but a positive way they accomplish for and in each other what we are here for, increasing the value and joy if life it also increases the support group to help. With my recovery. I have been working with support groups trying to help for about sixteen years now both in person and online. I have seen some of the greatest examples of human endurance and strength in so many of the people I get the opportunity to meet and work with. It is the groups that try to support the entire person and encourage each other that I think are the most successful because by being a social replacement for what many have lost in mobility. The group helps reestablish energy that so many have lost so much of. Being able to laugh even at yourself with each other's is such an important part of recovery. Some of the groups I have heard and attended are so matter of fact and what they think is professional the have lost the people touch and quickly lose people as well, they come to the meetings and feel worse at the end of the meeting is a sure way to lose people. Having people look forward to the next meeting shows you are doing what you said you started out to do help people. You can not help those who either can not or will not help themselves, so you must make a support meeting something they want to come back too and some thing that helps them see themselves and want to change to fit in better. That is the road to recovery wanting perhaps because this seems so philosophical, we need to look at it through the eyes of the here and now I have said I had a traumatic brain injury and except for anyone who has truly suffered one no one can appreciate all of the levels of your life that is affected by one. Our best medical and psychological doctors are barely scratching the surface of trying to deal with the myriad of symptoms that are a result. The treatments and recovery range from barbaric to bizarre. They try to portray themselves as professional which on many cases they are however if it were a mechanical issue, they can be extremely knowledgeable and, in many cases, capable of dealing with the deficits. Because they are attempting to deal with psychological feelings they fail miserably and, in many cases, damage the patients in a way that will slow or even prohibit their recovery. Of course, they would deny this or point out it is not an exact science. They are trying to do their best in a world that is not black and white but many shades. It took almost two years for a doctor to even recommend a support group to help. With my recovery. I have been working with support groups trying to help for about sixteen years now both in person and online. I have seen some of the greatest examples of human endurance and strength in so many of the people I get the opportunity to meet and work with. It is the groups that try to support the entire person and encourage each other that I think are the most successful because by being a social replacement for what many have lost in mobility. The group helps reestablish things that professionally do not seem as important such as humor, people begin to look forward to sharing not in a negative way but a positive growth way they accomplish for and in each other what we are here for, increasing the value and joy if life it also increases the energy that so many have lost so much of. To share the joy of living.

I hope you have seen in the book things that make you want to live as if you are in heaven now. Not wait till later. And that you understand that no one can give that to you it has to be chosen by you. If you are an agnostic, I hope you will step out of the thought that God existence is only important to how someone else views him and choose to embrace the fact that god is the father of all and you are here to raise the joy of the gift of the energy that is life. He wants you to make that worth the most it can be and the way to do that is with others who share your feelings. If you are an agnostic, I hope you will step out of the thought that god existence is only important to how someone else views him, and choose to embrace the fact that people who have and seek more enjoyment of the gift f life, not those who judge and by their judgement prohibit the increase of joy you and this place was created for.

While this book is about my vision it includes some of the conclusions, I drew from what I saw but I have tried to do the best that I could to tell them what I saw as instructed. I have seen many things since but all pale in comparison to the proof of life and existence and God. The rest are just all different reinforcements of this vision. They help me to put the experiences of my life in perspective. They are demonstrations of how God is the father of the fatherless truth. As I have told you in the final analysis your strength and your love and forgiveness are up to you, many don't think you can, but Jesus said can the son of man forgive sin? If you forgive yourself do not keep carrying it or you have not truly forgiven yourself.

CHAPTER 6

The End As You Know It

Many people talk about feelings, but they assume everyone will feel the same as they do. They do not consider that others have as much right as they do to decide what and how much they feel about anything. It seems they think everyone defines things the same way. You were given the authority to determine your own feelings because it gives you dominion over your own world. With that dominion it was necessary to have true justice, which is that you would be held accountable for what you said and did. It is the method that judges yourself. Since the beginning people have sought to have others see them as God, at least in the way they act. They understood force and control by that method. So, they quickly figured out convincing others that the joy of life comes from other people not what they choose, but what others choose for them. People are so convinced that it is others or society that determines how much joy in life you are permitted to have. It has gotten to the point that because they have feelings, yet they are told it comes from with out instead of from within. Since value is what someone else allows you to have, the way to control them is to take value from them and give it to someone else. This is socialism it holds society to be your god and people have allowed it to destroy whole countries. You see what you allow to dictate to you that you should value you give your life to. Since you have permitted what can not feel what you feel you have submitted to a lie that can not know your feelings so there is no value to them of your feelings. They will continue to violate you if you allow it. Once there is no concern for your feelings, things are reduced to the level of such a low level that there is no justice possible. Because the only true justice like your feelings begin from within you. As a result, after these many years of this slow progression of the loss of value people are almost powerless to stand up to what divides. Each society manipulates and reduces the value of the individual to where we are today. Because they have committed so much to the external pressures, they have lost most of the internal strength that will be needed as society chases value that they have lost so many more will be hurt that in order to maintain power they use distraction through war and civil disturbance. This constant progression of loss and the increase of suffering has gotten to the point that people are becoming immune to this form of control. so, people are being forced to search themselves for strength in a world that has gone wild. This will either increase the speed of loss that occurs to control the people and it will increase the need people have to know and find God within themselves. So, in order to avoid the judgement of other people will withdraw within themselves since that is the only place they will find strength. As the recent events have taught you can be physically present and yet not there engaged. This is the rapture of which people speak of. People say God will send his army and force all to be obedient, although he has never acted that way, he sent Jesus and yet hid him for years, yet this time he is going to send an army as though you could physically contend with spirit. The reality of it is what he said thousand of years ago people will not see the second coming until it has done what it was intended to do. What is that? To summon in the judgement day as we call it. The fact that everyone judges themselves every second of their lives. Only they know why they did what they did and why, for the most what they did. But since we think in terms of time because of our physical presence which requires space time but God and spirit and intelligence does not require days or time as we know it neither does your feelings because when you choose things that divide and separate and loses value you feel it. So, there is no single day that is judgement there is a day when you will receive what you have judged yourself worthy of receiving. As we move forward there will be more wars and civil unrest. Because people and nations need to define value, they will seek to attack others that seem to have more civil peace and perhaps order that they think will be something they can show their people that is value they can give others. It will be not only the result of socialist nations but, those nations that are run by people who value only money as the sole measure of wealth. And the people who have allowed themselves to be divided by race, financial status, religious doctrine and even education, since it is socially motivated. This variety of external forces will speed up the social failure. So, between those who have turned to internal searching and those who have removed them selves as these things progress people will begin to see that the false god of society is causing the loss of so much value including the death of our children for no gain that people will search and discover new words that convey the same truth that they will begin to refuse to sacrifice their children or families to the false god of society. It will increase the speed of people deciding what they are committing to. Again, a form of judgement day. If the people do not find the strength to quit sacrificing their children and families, the destruction of all is guaranteed because they do not value others. Even the use of all of our new weapons will not destroy everyone because we are not dinosaurs and God gave us dominion. The survivors will begin to seek the truth not what someone says buy what it is to them. This is the path that so many of the world's elite choose but it still requires you to permit it. There are those who have no concept of the value of the gift of life and have no intention of raising it. I know many would think this impossible, how many millionaires commit suicide? How many societies push the division of races? How many churches teach one way but do not do what Jesus said? How long do people think that they can limit God by saying what they think he can and can not do? If God created all it means he created all of the sides not just the ones, you think or recognize.

I know you want to know the day hour and minute, but like all things it is already done the reason for that is while people get to choose to raise the value of life or throw it away, God is good and will always lead to more. In all things he increases and while we can choose to limit ourselves God never will. Even when we think of loss, everything we define just adds more even loss must come from somewhere else, more is there. The purpose of this creation is to increase the glory of God. We are given the choice to be part of, or away from God. As Jesus said in the beginning, I was in my father my father is in me and we are one. I submit to you your finger is in you and it performs your will but if you cut it off it is still in you, but you are no longer in it however there is documentation that you can sometimes still feel it. God is connected by intent and energy so unlike the severed finger if you seek to do his will you are one. Jesus knew all of this and taught you how to live by seeing through our fathers' eyes.

So, like feelings are the domain of the individual, so too is judgement. Because it is only truly relevant to the individual not the social group. So, I believe the time has come for each individual to judge themselves, what that means is that only each and every one must show what they stand for. For this to happen you have a choice. In keeping with the order that God created and the method he has used you must do also it does not call for violence, in fact violence removes the value it should produce. When you are in a situation that either someone is supporting and espousing a lie turn your back on them. If your political leaders do not do what is right for all the people which is, grant them the freedom to judge themselves by what they do, not hold others responsible to pay and reward their failure. Then whenever confronted with them turn your back to them. If they pass in a motorcade or on foot turn your back to them. Do not engage or support them anywhere especially in your vote. IF your religious institution does not address and support all of Gods children who have committed themselves to God.

As they know him but maintain that they are not going to be in heaven because they are not doing what the church says they must they are putting themselves above God by judging his children. But if that person does not judge themselves in a manner that does not support the freedom god gave each then they have judged themselves. Hold them accountable for what they did, not what someone else says they did. Your form of showing in every circumstance is to turn your back and disengage with them if they are a true friend or even family member they will seek you out later, so you can tell them why you felt the need to disengage. If it is an educator or political person turn your back on them. Unless they can provide irrefutable proof of the truth in every situation, if there are contraindications and it is not true in every situation it is not the whole truth.

This is both examples of how your judgement day

and your rapture are truly one and the same, each time you fail to turn your back because your internal feelings told you should, you are violating yourself and will lose because you disappoint yourself. If you fail to teach your children not to violate themselves, they will follow illegal orders and fail to protect the people they should. If they follow orders that violate the freedoms of others to commit to what they believe if it harms no one. There will always be those who seek to destroy true value so if you see one of theses point them out to the police for, they sought to destroy the value of your protest. Violence if necessary will come from God not from men. Stand for respect of your flag and all those who gave their lives to provide what they thought it stood for to them. Each time you fail to peacefully turn your back to someone who stands for division or the reduction of true value, you turn your back on God however you know or define him. You are here to judge yourself not each other so if you do not turn your back on those who supports lies and the loss of value, you fail God. While others may not see as you do you are not called for them you are for you. If you do not do this, you support those who have no value for you or your family and it is a green light for them to continue sacrificing your children to the will of other men. Those who died for the American flag died for the freedom it was supposed to stand for our leaders have continually violated that trust and the people have allowed it because they don't see value or at least true value. The fact that what they value is subject to the confidence of others that they can deliver something of true value to back up their form of value, currency once that confidence fails their value fails. On the other hand, Gods value is based in feelings you each get individually and carry with you throughout your entire life. You can not avoid or not feel so it does not need your confidence or approval. So even in this life you suffer with feelings you can not avoid but will feel always. So, his value is self-contained, so your choice to seek to be part of his will that the children use their own will to serve him by serving each other the freedom he gave them. This is the reward you receive now and forever. If you violate his gift to you, it will be taken from you. So, your choice judges you and only you. It is not subject to what others say or do. If you turn your back you disengage which is like disappearing, that is how you are raptured. But you have to be willing to stand for God not for what others say. It has to begin today and it will increase you interaction with god.

CHAPTER 7

So It Begins, It Is Finished

I have told you repeatedly that time and space relate to the physical part of you. Your energy and soul are part of the energy of God. They are not connected to time and space but, they still create physical feelings. Those feelings are the result of how you judge yourself by what you choose to think has value to you. Since the purpose of this creation is to increase the energy which comes through the good feelings you get. It has been necessary to allow us to have the freedom to choose, but with that freedom came the right to learn and to learn allows us to forgive ourselves. We have not learned and are supporting worldwide the elimination of the freedom we were given in favor of the false god of society. We have given up the glory of the gift of dominion that God gave us when he allowed the individual to choose what and how much they should feel about anything. This is what you have given the God of men socialism. You are worth what they say you are worth. You have thrown away the gifts 0f the lives of all who have fought for freedom. You have totally negated their gift; you have made their deaths meaningless by supporting the thing they died trying to protect you from. You have chosen to be the slaves of public opinion. Welcome to your self-imposed slavery. Let those who have died and you have turned into sacrifice live in you every second of every day. In addition, when the politicians seek to distract you from the unjust causes and pilfering they are doing by sending your sons and daughters to die for their lust may they haunt every second of your everyday. When they send the armed forces and law enforcement to pillage your homes remember you voted for them and gave them your power to do what they will. While the news media rants and raves about select racial or socioeconomic issues to keep you divide think of how many things you bought from the sponsors of them. While you weep at home over your losses remember you gave them the authority to do these things. You accused each other instead of the leaders that orchestrated it in wall street and the capital buildings everywhere. You allowed the news media unchecked to incite violence to show how above it they all are. You never questioned their motives. They played you as a fool and you allowed it thinking God or someone else will protect you from yourself. But you are now going to learn the true meaning of mercy. You will receive what you sought. All of the misery you sought for others is yours now. You can wait for others to tell you what you feel if that is what you want to but the judgement has always been. However, you have been shielded from so much of it. Now you will receive what you sought. You are given to your brethren since that is who you have chosen. May the one hundred million people who have disappeared in the reeducation camps in Russia and China and their tears be with you every second. May the billions of people that have died over the name of something they could not even conceive of let alone name or define haunt you night and day since your media and leaders say it is just a myth. Let your leaders and media tell you the number of lost children they eagerly reported on the death of may the tears and the groans of their loved ones echo in your mind night and day. Continue to elect who the media and Wall Street parade before you even though they have not a single answer but will do what the media and their financial handlers say to do including political parties that exist by division. Watch your children die on the television sets. You who stand for nothing but worship what other men say may you reap the rewards of your disgrace. I am calling the dead to raise in your life so you will know existence is not dependent on men. You want to see others suffer I say join those who suffer. It is not what I want or the wish of the father it is and always has been your choice. God does not need to use force you are perfectly capable of making each other miserable, you are well practiced at it. He just will show the mercy of allowing you to receive what you wished for others.

The point of this creation is to always increase the energy that is God positive and negative will always increase you have gotten to choose which you would be. the negative will exist in a place like we all have a box or drawer we hid things we liked or somehow gave us value, most of the time it sat there almost forgotten never to be seen or touched again. Those who have chosen to be apart from but not with the rest will be that drawer. Their tears and interaction not allowed. But at least they judged themselves so too will it be with you. Just as the tree of knowledge of good and evil in heaven no one wants what can only always be less than and not the whole. Once the remaining people that are here choose to be part of and treat, everyone as part of with the right God gave them to have dominion in their own existence heaven will be here. But before that you need to learn this lesson for all time. Work always to increase never to divide take what is divided and find ways to make it useful in creating more. If there is no answer, ask the father if there is still no answer turn your back on it is not for you. Do not say you will and then vote to give it power.

What is going to be now the corrupt people you have elected and supported will continue to distract and divide this nation and every nation there will be continued war until the people see and know this truth then there will be what many call the rapture people will do what I have told you here. They will begin to turn their back on those who divide or attempt to divide us. It will grow to a point that people will encourage each other to not engage or support those who seek to divide and weaken us. It will get to the point that law enforcement and the military will refuse illegal orders and refuse to fire on crowds that are nonviolent and not only willing to but eagerly point out and hand over anyone who destroys the value of their protest this will force the politician's to seek other means to punish the public which will only feed and convince those who do not understand that their excess must be curbed. Lobbying will be banned, and term limits enforced. It will again become an obligation to each other to work for the good of all. This will occur on a worldwide basis. It must because heaven can only exist for those who allow it for all. People will finally realize that true value comes from within not the will or consent of others. And that to harm the least of them will harm all.

I know you want to know hour and day watch the news listen to your heart and your neighbors it is already underway. I know you want miracles this is a miracle and what you will get. To understand in truth, sacrifice and mercy. To be able to identify evil at its earliest stages. to know the correct way to handle it. To know what is going on and coming, I would submit that is a miracle since it has been the same since the beginning and never laid out like this. It also does not remove anything by force and while suggesting we have the power to limit everything does not magically remove anything but puts it in the place the creator intended. You choose it always comes down to that, in a place where angels fear to tread, not because of death but of harming one who could choose to be saved.

Why should you concern yourself with doing anything, if you only knew the number of inhabitants of Sodom, and Gomorrah, that said the same thing? No ruler or govt or leader has any power but what you give them. If they would have turned their acks and shunned the evil doers, they would not have met the fate they did. If you vote for and support the corrupt governments and politicians, they will be corrupt. You cry for justice; justice is holding you accountable for what you did AND did not do. If you do nothing you will meet the same fate for to do nothing is to eliminate the consequences of evil, that makes YOU a supporter of evil. If it is to be destroyed, you must be destroyed with it since it could not exist without you allowing it. Just as mercy rewards your judgement of what you value so justice rewards the judgment of the evil doers to receive what they did. So, you must be involved not by judging the individual but by the results of what they said or did. Justice is not supporting or allowing evil around you. Therefore, you see today people think that the history of Sodom and Gomorrah is so harsh, yet they want divine intervention, when it occurs they are aghast at the brutality of it. Be careful what you wish for. You do not need to fight the lords' battles but don't try to conduct them either, you will not like the results. This place was given to the sons of men, if they make a mess of it the father will not clean their mess, if you continue to cry out instead of shunning evil you will get the same thing and in a manner that will never be forgotten.

In the bible it talks about the tribes of Israel and one of these tribes were great archers. They never sinned, or missed the mark, that is what sin is missing the mark god has in your life that when you hit it the rewards are overflowing. If you miss that mark unintentionally you can be forgiven but you still receive the consequences of missing the mark that is mercy. If you missed the mark because you didn't try or care that is sacrifice, it just cost you the value hitting the mark would provide. Only you know that you did not try, but all f the rewards and accolades will never be there for you. You say you are only human I was human as well, why do you call me lord and do not what I say? Is it because you think I would give you a task that cannot be done? If you have no faith you will not find the place, I have prepared for you that will shield you from what is to come. In order to have that place you need to know beyond a shadow of a doubt that you are the fathers and he would not harm what is his, so whatever comes it will not remove you from the rest of what will be, but you can choose to throw it away and if you do you will receive what you chose.

CPSIA information can be obtained
at www.ICGtesting.com
Printed in the USA
BVHW041156070722
641568BV00015B/767/J

9 781669 834588